Wisconsin

By Lisa Trumbauer

Consultant

Nanci R. Vargus, Ed.D.
Assistant Professor of Literacy
University of Indianapolis, Indianapolis, Indiana

Children's Press®
A Division of Scholastic Inc.
New York   Toronto   London   Auckland   Sydney
Mexico City   New Delhi   Hong Kong
Danbury, Connecticut

Designer: Herman Adler Design
Photo Researcher: Caroline Anderson
The photo on the cover shows Little Manitou Falls, Pattison State Park.

Library of Congress Cataloging-in-Publication Data
Trumbauer, Lisa, 1963-
 Wisconsin / by Lisa Trumbauer.
  p. cm. — (Rookie read-about geography)
Includes index.
Summary: A simple introduction to the geography and people
  of Wisconsin.
 ISBN 0-516-22745-9 (lib. bdg.)   0-516-23607-5 (pbk.)
 1. Wisconsin—Juvenile literature. 2. Wisconsin—Geography—Juvenile
literature. [1. Wisconsin.] I. Title. II. Series.
 F581.3.T78 2003
 977.5-dc21   C - 1
                          2003003898

CHILDREN'S PRESS, and ROOKIE READ-ABOUT®,
and associated logos are trademarks and or registered trademarks
of Scholastic Library Publishing. SCHOLASTIC and associated logos
are trademarks and or registered trademarks of Scholastic Inc.
1 2 3 4 5 6 7 8 9 10 R 12 11 10 09 08 07 06 05 04 03

Do you know which state makes the most cheese?

Wisconsin does!

Can you find Wisconsin
on this map? It is part of
a region (REE-juhn) called
the Midwest. Four states and
two Great Lakes border it.

CANADA

WASHINGTON

OREGON

IDAHO

MONTANA

NORTH DAKOTA

SOUTH DAKOTA

WYOMING

NEBRASKA

MINNESOTA

WISCONSIN

MICHIGAN

IOWA

NEW HAMPSHIRE

VERMONT

MAINE

NEW YORK

MASSACHUSETTS

RHODE ISLAND

CONNECTICUT

NEW JERSEY

PENNSYLVANIA

DELAWARE

NEVADA

UTAH

CALIFORNIA

COLORADO

KANSAS

ILLINOIS

INDIANA

OHIO

WEST VIRGINIA

MARYLAND

Washington, D.C.

MISSOURI

KENTUCKY

VIRGINIA

ARIZONA

NEW MEXICO

OKLAHOMA

ARKANSAS

TENNESSEE

NORTH CAROLINA

SOUTH CAROLINA

TEXAS

MISSISSIPPI

ALABAMA

GEORGIA

LOUISIANA

FLORIDA

North

West   East

South

ALASKA   CANADA

MEXICO

HAWAII

Wisconsin is sometimes called "America's dairyland." It has more than 75,000 farms.

Many of these farms raise dairy cows. Milk comes from dairy cows.

Farmers in Wisconsin
also grow green beans,
cranberries, and other crops.

Cranberries

Green beans

Milwaukee is Wisconsin's biggest city. It is on Lake Michigan.

Over half a million people live in Milwaukee.

11

Madison is Wisconsin's capital. It was named after the fourth president of the United States. His name was James Madison.

The capitol building was
built to look like the United
States Capitol building.

Many people in Wisconsin work in manufacturing (man-yuh-FAK-chur-ing). This means they make things.

Most people make food products, wood and paper products, car parts, and machines.

Harley-Davidson is a type of motorcycle (MOH-tur-sye-kuhl). These motorcycles were first built in Milwaukee in 1903.

Today, the Harley-Davidson is one of the most popular motorcycles in the world.

Many people cheer for the
Green Bay Packers football
team. Green Bay is a town
to the south of Green Bay.

19

Wisconsin also has many lakes. People enjoy fishing and water sports on the lakes.

Otter

You might see deer or
otters near the lakes, too.

In northern Wisconsin, you can visit the Apostle (uh-POSS-uhl) Islands National Lakeshore.

These islands are in Lake Superior. You will see many lighthouses there.

Western Wisconsin has cliffs and forests. Black bears and other animals live in the forests.

The robin is the state bird.

Some of the best cheese is
made in Monroe County.

Every summer, in Little Chute, there is a big cheese festival.

Maybe someday you can visit Wisconsin. You can see the farms, forests, lakes, and lighthouses.

Don't forget to try the cheese!

Words You Know

cheese

cows

cranberries

Green Bay Packers

30

Harley-Davidson

lighthouse

robin

Index

About the Author

Lisa Trumbauer has written nearly 200 books for children. She lives with her husband, two cats, and one dog in Hillsborough, New Jersey. She loves to travel and write about the United States.

Photo Credits

Photographs © 2003: AP/Wide World Photos: 18, 30 bottom right (Morry Gash), 17, 31 top left (Pat Goddard); Art Resource, NY/Reunion des Musees Nationaux: 12 (photo by Arnaudet); Corbis Images: 16 (Bettmann), 15 (Layne Kennedy), 21 (Mary Ann McDonald), 29 (Randy Miller), 20 (Phil Schermeister); Corbis SABA/Ralf-Finn Hestoft: 8, 30 bottom left; Envision: 9 (B.W. Hoffmann), 3, 30 top left (Osentoski & Zoda); Great Western Cheese Festival: 27; ImageState/Mark Gibson: 11; Lynn M. Stone: 6, 30 top right; Photo Researchers, NY: 26 (David R. Frazier), 13 (Arvind Garg), 25, 31 bottom (Mr. M.H. Sharp); Terry Donnelly: cover, 23, 24, 31 top right.

Maps by Bob Italiano